KEEP IT UP, CUTIE!

xo!
Anna Paz

keep IT UP, CUTiE!

A NOT-QUITE SELF-HELP BOOK

ANNA PRZY

ILLUSTRATED BY NIC FARRELL

RIZZOLI UNIVERSE

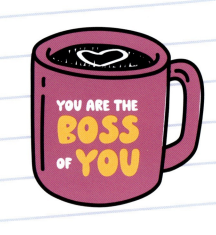

YOU ARE THE
BOSS
OF **YOU**

KEEP
IT UP,
CUTIE

INTRODUCTION

Writing a book always felt like something I didn't deserve to do—it was something for serious people who have something important to say. Then one day I woke up and realized I did have something important to say. Every time I helped someone by talking about an experience, an awkward feeling, my daily struggle, or overcoming some mental hurdle, I was writing this book.

Now these messages of hope and encouragement live on a page where you can read one anytime you need to. Life is hard, messy, sad, amazing, challenging, and everything in between. I'm just here to help you feel a little less alone along the way.

CHAPTER 1

EVERYTHING IS MADE UP

Do you feel like you have to live your life on some kind of timeline? I'm a fully grown adult woman who recently realized that I have been in a lifelong race with myself to nowhere.

THE TIMELINE IS NOT REAL. There is no right order to move through your lifetime. You aren't failing. You can't fail at something that doesn't exist.

If it feels like your life events are backing up on the timeline, that's not really a thing. You can reach whatever milestones you want on the timeline you make for you.

YOU'RE NOT LATE FOR ANYTHING, CUTIE, AND DON'T LET ANYBODY MAKE YOU FEEL THAT WAY.

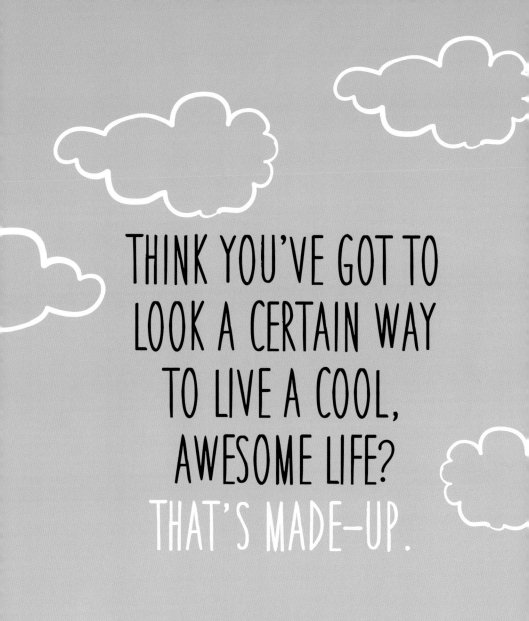

THINK YOU'VE GOT TO LOOK A CERTAIN WAY TO LIVE A COOL, AWESOME LIFE? THAT'S MADE-UP.

THAT PRESSURE YOU FEEL TO DO MORE
AND BE MORE? MADE-UP. STOP
SUBSCRIBING TO THE SOCIETAL SHIT
THAT MAKES YOU FEEL LIKE YOU'RE
LESS-THAN AND START SUBSCRIBING
TO WHATEVER MAKES YOUR HEART
FEEL LIKE YOU JUST HAD YOUR
FAVORITE FANCY COFFEE ON YOUR
FAVORITE WEATHER DAY IN YOUR
FAVORITE COMFY OUTFIT.

ON THOSE DAYS WHEN YOU WAKE UP
FEELIN' WEIRD, JUST REMEMBER:
YOU CAN BE WHOEVER YOU WANNA
BE. YOU CAN CHANGE YOUR MIND
EVERY SINGLE DAY. THERE ARE NO
RULES AGAINST IT. YOUR BRAIN
DOESN'T EVEN HAVE ARMS, SO
STOP LETTING IT PUSH YOU INTO
STUFF OR HOLD YOU BACK.

I GOTTA BE HONEST WITH YOU—I DON'T REALLY WANT TO DO TODAY. SO LET'S KEEP IT EASY LIKE SUNDAY MORNING—NOT MY SUNDAY MORNING, BECAUSE I HAVE SUNDAY SCARIES—EASY LIKE SOMEBODY ELSE'S SUNDAY MORNING. OKAY? THANK YOU.

YOU DON'T HAVE TO JUST SUCK IT UP. JUST BECAUSE YOU CAN GET THROUGH IT, DOESN'T MEAN YOU SHOULD. TAKE A LOAD OFF, CUTIE.

EVERYTHING IS FAKE
AND NOTHING MATTERS

The systems are
designed to keep
us down

EVERYTHING IS
MADE UP

SO EAT THE
CHEESEBURGER

DO YOU FEEL LOST ON THE ROAD OF LIFE? HAVE YOU CONSIDERED YOU MIGHT BE MOVING IN THE WRONG DIRECTION?

STOP MOVING TOWARD MORE.

Look for an easier route. Maybe one that leads to peace, contentment, and simplicity instead. Travel your own road, bestie. You're not less-than if you want less. Even if you're taking the tiniest steps, you're still moving in the right direction.

THERE ARE PEOPLE WHO ARE NOT GONNA GET YOU—THEY JUST AREN'T. **THEY'LL NEVER SEE THAT YOU ARE AS CHERISHED AS A CHICKEN FINGER, AS MAGNIFICENT AS MACARONI.** STOP USING ALL THAT ENERGY TRYING TO MAKE THEM SEE YOUR VALUE. USE THAT ENERGY ON SOMEBODY WHO GETS YOU AS EXACTLY AS YOU ARE.

I DON'T HAVE THE TIME OR THE ENERGY OR THE PATIENCE FOR ANY SHENANIGANS THIS WEEK. SO LET'S JUST KEEP IT COOL AND CALM AND CASUAL, OKAY? THANK YOU.

IT'S CALLED MANIFESTING—LOOK IT UP.

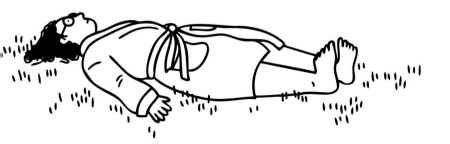

When you change your definitions, you change your life. Here are some things I've redefined:

Potential:

I see my potential is to be the least unhappy I can possibly be.

Productivity:

Rest is productive, being kind to yourself is productive, eating a tasty snack is productive.

Success:

I'm successfully not as miserable as I used to be!

Giving 100%:

If all you have is 10%, then giving 10% is giving 100%.

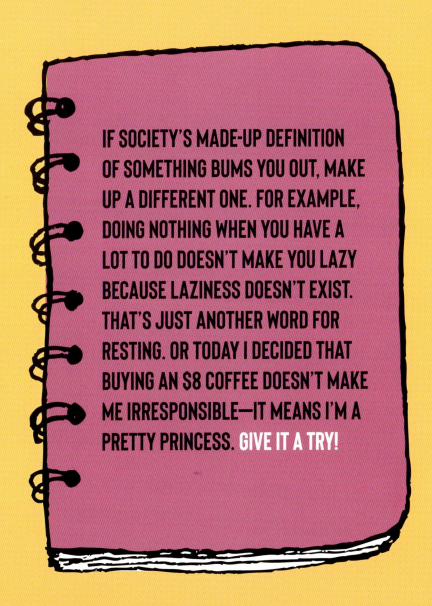

IF SOCIETY'S MADE-UP DEFINITION OF SOMETHING BUMS YOU OUT, MAKE UP A DIFFERENT ONE. FOR EXAMPLE, DOING NOTHING WHEN YOU HAVE A LOT TO DO DOESN'T MAKE YOU LAZY BECAUSE LAZINESS DOESN'T EXIST. THAT'S JUST ANOTHER WORD FOR RESTING. OR TODAY I DECIDED THAT BUYING AN $8 COFFEE DOESN'T MAKE ME IRRESPONSIBLE—IT MEANS I'M A PRETTY PRINCESS. **GIVE IT A TRY!**

CHAPTER 2

BURNT THE FUCK OUT?

ARE YOU *conflicted* BECAUSE YOU WERE RAISED TO BELIEVE THAT YOUR SELF-WORTH WAS TIED TO YOUR PRODUCTIVITY?

But now you know that isn't true and you want something else for your life? Hi, I'm a fully grown adult woman who finally knows that I am valuable simply because I exist. I want to stop doing things that don't make me happy, but my brain is fighting my heart every step of the way. *I feel like there are two people inside me —and there's a battle raging and nobody is winning.*

BAD DAY REMINDER

UNLEARNING A LIFETIME OF HUSTLE CULTURE IS VERY HARD. BUT TRYING IS BETTER THAN NOT TRYING.

HEY, I OVERDID IT. I SAID YES TO *WAY* TOO MANY THINGS WHEN I WAS HAVING A GOOD DAY AND NOW I'M PAST MY LIMIT. I DON'T WANT TO DO ANY MORE THINGS, OKAY? NO MORE THINGS, EXCEPT MAYBE LYING ON A FLUFFY BLANKET AND EATING SOME CHIPS, OKAY? THANK YOU.

DO YOU TREAT YOUR ENTIRE LIFE LIKE A CHECKLIST?

I'VE SPENT MY ENTIRE LIFE MOVING FROM ONE TASK TO THE NEXT. WHEN I GOT TO THE END OF THE CHECKLIST, ALL I HAD LEFT WAS THE CRUSHING REALITY OF NOT KNOWING ONE GODDAMN THING ABOUT MYSELF. WHO AM I? I DON'T KNOW, BUT LOOK HOW PRODUCTIVE I WAS? BUILDING AN ENTIRE LIFE AROUND CHECKING OFF THE NEXT THING IS NOT SUSTAINABLE. IF YOU HAVEN'T ALREADY, BESTIE, SET ASIDE THE CHECKLIST EVERY ONCE IN A WHILE. THERE'S NO PRIZE AT THE END. IT'S TIME TO STOP CHECKING AND START LIVING INSTEAD.

THAT THING YOU'RE TRYING SO HARD TO MAKE WORK? IT DOESN'T HAVE TO WORK. IF YOU DON'T FEEL UP TO IT, YOU DON'T HAVE TO DO IT. AT LEAST PUT "NOT WORKING" AS ONE OF THE OPTIONS IN YOUR BRAIN. AND THAT THING WILL TAKE AS LONG AS IT TAKES. THIS APPLIES TO LITERALLY EVERYTHING—IT TAKES AS LONG AS IT TAKES. YOU CAN'T MAKE IT GO FASTER BY WILLING IT SO!

SOMETIMES ACCEPTANCE IS BLISS, BESTIE.

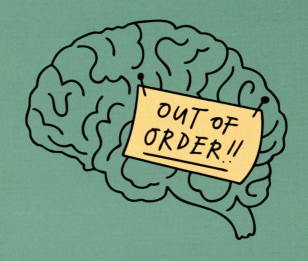

You cannot overachieve your way out of burnout.

YOU SHOULD NOT—I REPEAT—YOU SHOULD NOT IGNORE ALL THE WARNING SIGNS THAT YOU ARE HEADED FOR A BREAKDOWN. IF YOU GIVE MORE THAN 100% OF YOURSELF FOR DAYS ON END, YOU WILL BREAK.

BURN

ADDITIONALLY, ONCE YOU'RE
BURNT OUT, YOU CANNOT OVER-
ACHIEVE YOUR WAY THROUGH
HEALING EITHER. WHEN I IGNORED
BOTH MY BODY AND MY MIND
SCREAMING AT ME TO STOP, I
COULDN'T GET OUT OF BED FOR DAYS.

*So do as I say,
not as I did, cutie.*

OUT

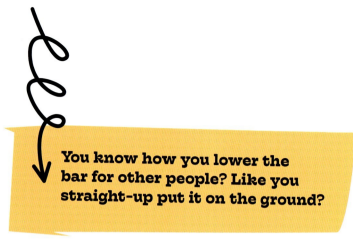

You know how you lower the bar for other people? Like you straight-up put it on the ground?

So why is the bar for you way up here? And why do you punish yourself harder than anybody else for not reaching it? No more of that.

You are the keeper of you. How about a little more compassion for you? You wouldn't beat up a friend for whatever you're beating yourself up about.

YOU OWE YOURSELF THE LOVE YOU GIVE OTHER PEOPLE.

YOU ARE THE BOSS OF YOU, SO BE A GOOD ONE.

I LOST SOME OF MY OOMPH, YOU KNOW? I DIDN'T HAVE THE MOST OOMPH, BUT I HAD MORE THAN A SQUISHY, OLD POTATO. SO I'M GONNA NEED IT BACK. I'M GONNA NEED A LITTLE PEP IN THE STEP. I'M GONNA NEED, LIKE, A LITTLE RAZZLE IN MY DAZZLE, OKAY? THANK YOU.

JUST BECAUSE YOU'RE GOOD AT DOING SOME-THING DOESN'T MEAN YOU ENJOY DOING IT. TAKE A LIFE INVENTORY, BESTIE. IS IT REALLY SERVING YOU?

We get stuck in this "no pain, no gain" mindset when it comes to our lives. We put higher value on doing the hard things. But often you're trying to achieve that hard thing from a place of fear. That's no way to live, bestie!

There's no shame in taking the easier route. It's okay to choose something that might not be the hardest and do it slowly. You don't have to hustle, and you don't have to do it for somebody else.

Turn that outside noise off.

GOT NOTHIN' IN

WOO-WOO

NOTHIN' IN THE

NOTHIN' IN THE

WOO-WOO

Nothin' in the

Nothin' in the

AWOOOO

Nothin' in the

strength -to-act

around - people

I'M COMPLETELY

44

THE TANK

ENERGY TANK

TANK

emotional tank

tank

musterin'-up-my-
-like-a-human-
tank

AND TOTALLY ON E.

Are you having trouble successfully juggling all the balls in your life and things are slipping because you're the kind of person who thinks they can do it all? Plus, you're absolutely petrified of ever disappointing anybody, ever? It might be a sign that there are too many balls in your court.

WHEN THIS IS HAPPENING, IT'S REALLY IMPORTANT TO REMEMBER YOU.

STOP DROPPING THE BALL OF YOUR NEEDS FIRST WHEN YOU'RE STRUGGLING IN OTHER AREAS OF YOUR LIFE.

YOUR NEEDS STILL MATTER.

PUT DOWN A DIFFERENT BALL AND TAKE CARE OF YOU.

SO FOR THIS WEEK I'M ACTUALLY ALL DONE. IF YOU WERE THINKING ABOUT PUTTING ANYTHING ELSE ON MY PLATE, I WON'T BE DOING IT. MAYBE WE'LL JUST REGROUP NEXT WEEK. I'LL LET YOU KNOW HOW I'M DOING AND IF I'M READY TO DO STUFF AGAIN, OKAY? THANK YOU.

CHAPTER 3

FEEL YOUR FEELINGS

TODAY IS TESTING ME.
I DIDN'T STUDY, SO IF I
COULD GET LIKE A CHEAT
SHEET OR A FREE PASS, IT
WOULD BE FUCKIN' SUPER,
OKAY? THANK YOU.

Do you keep saying that "everything's fine" even though everything is not fine? Sometimes when we squash our feelings down, they just get bigger. That's a lot of pressure on you as well as a lot of extra energy being used to cover up what you could be trying to sort through instead.

You don't have to put on a brave face all the time, and you don't have to have it all together.

IT'S OKAY TO BE LESS THAN PERFECT. IT'S OKAY TO ASK FOR HELP. GETTING OVER OR THROUGH SOMETHING TAKES AS LONG AS IT TAKES. RUSHING YOURSELF IS JUST ADDED PRESSURE. BUT TRY TO FACE WHAT'S NOT FINE.

AND GIVE YOURSELF A LITTLE KISS AND A TREAT, 'CAUSE YOU'VE GOT THIS.

NOTHING is wrong but

I'M DISCONTENT BUT I

I'm a little bit SAD

I CAN'T PUT A FINGER ON

I'M NOT SURE

if I HAVE THE ENERGY to

EVERYING feels off.

♩ ♩

DON'T KNOW _WHAT ABOUT_

but I can't pinpoint **WHY**

WHAT I WANT OR NEED

EVEN IF I KNOW

DO ANYTHING ABOUT IT.

ON HEAVY DAYS, DON'T FORGET THAT YOUR NEEDS STILL MATTER.

BRUSH YOUR TEETH.

DRINK SOME WATER.

HAVE A MEAL.

MOVE YOUR BODY.

CHANGE YOUR CLOTHES.

TAKE YOUR MEDS.

BREATHE.

DO ONE THING JUST FOR YOU!

PET THAT PUPPY.

DO THAT CRAFT.

GO TO THAT PARK.

YOU DON'T HAVE TO CHASE HAPPINESS. IT'S NOT A DESTINATION— IT'S JUST A PART OF THE RACE EVERY ONCE IN A WHILE.

On those days when you wake up and everything seems impossible and you're dreading everything, TRY ONE THING:

Stop thinking big-picture, like "I've got the whole day ahead of me," and start thinking "I think I can change my pants."

OBJECTS IN MOTION TEND TO STAY IN MOTION, AND THAT GOES FOR YOU TOO, BESTIE. SO TRY ONE THING, AND IT MIGHT LEAD TO TWO OR THREE THINGS. IT DOESN'T HURT TO TRY ONE THING. AND IF IT DOESN'T WORK, PLEASE, FOR THE LOVE OF GRILLED CHEESE SANDWICHES, DON'T BEAT YOURSELF UP. BECAUSE YOU TRIED.

I'M NOT ACTUALLY GONNA BE EXHAUSTED ANYMORE, OKAY? I JUST WANNA FEEL LIKE ONE MILLION DOLLARS. AND I'M GONNA BE AN EASY-BREEZY CAREFREE PERSON FROM HERE ON OUT. OKAY? THANK YOU.

Do you feel guilty when . . . YES! You didn't need to finish that sentence. I feel guilty and anxious about everything all the time. So whatever you were gonna say, I know the answer is YES.

I FEEL LIKE I AM CONSTANTLY FAILING EVERYONE AROUND ME, INCLUDING MYSELF.

I FEEL GUILTY THAT I'M NOT ABLE TO TAKE ON MORE AT WORK.

I FEEL LIKE I HAVE NEVER KNOWN PEACE.

IT'S OKAY NOT TO KNOW WHO YOU ARE OR WHAT YOU WANT. NOT HAVING A STRONG SENSE OF SELF OR PURPOSE DOES NOT MAKE YOU DIRECTIONLESS. YOU ARE NOT LOST—YOU'RE LIVING.

EVERY DAY YOU ARE LEARNING, LIVING, GROWING, AND CHANGING. HOW CAN WE CONCRETELY KNOW THAT WHAT'S RIGHT FOR TODAY IS ALSO RIGHT FOR TOMORROW?

Why are you worrying about what you're gonna do for the rest of your life? You're here, and it's now. This is it. This is what we've got. Try to have some fun and do some good stuff.

Ta-da!

Now you've got direction and purpose.

FEEL YOUR

You deserve to feel your feelings.

FEELINGS,

You don't need to power through it.

BESTIE. YOU

You don't need to pretend you're okay.

HAVE THEM

You don't need to keep it to yourself.

FOR A REASON.

BAD DAY REMINDER

ON YOUR WORST DAYS,
REMEMBER THAT YOUR
SURVIVAL RATE OF
YOUR WORST DAYS
SO FAR IS 100%, SO
OUR ODDS FOR THIS ONE
ARE PRETTY GOOD TOO.

THERE ARE TIMES WHEN I DON'T LET MYSELF BELIEVE THAT I'M STRONG AND BRAVE BECAUSE I KNOW THAT THERE ARE OTHER PEOPLE OUT THERE WHO ARE STRONGER AND BRAVER. BUT THAT'S NOT HOW STRENGTH WORKS.

I'm a badass between my mental, physical, and emotional limits. And you're a

badass

within your limits. Whether you think you're strong and brave or not, you're still here and that's amazing.

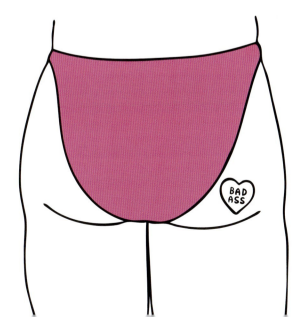

BAD ASS

CHAPTER 4

BE A KICKASS LITTLE HOTTIE

Sometimes I struggle with my body. Not the inside stuff—the skin suit. So here is a reminder for both you and me: Our bodies, while cute as heckaroni and cheese, are just vessels for all the other things that we are.

We've survived every single day of our lives so far. This skin suit carried us every step of the way. All of the important things that made us laugh and smile—we experienced them in these skin suits.

So whether it is a good day or bad day for the skin suit, always remember who you are: a kickass little hottie.

I'VE DECIDED THAT THIS DAY IS GONNA BLOW MY MIND. EXISTENTIAL DREAD? NOT FOR ME. I'M GONNA KICK THIS DAY IN THE FACE, AND I'M GONNA TELL ANYTHING THAT'S PISSING ME OFF TO SMOOCH MY CABOOSE. AND YOU KNOW WHAT? COWAFUCKINGBUNGA, YOU KNOW? THANK YOU.

IS A CERTAIN SPACE IN YOUR LIFE
STARTING TO FEEL UNCOMFY? MAYBE
IT'S BECAUSE IT DOESN'T FIT ANYMORE.
MAYBE IT'S TIME FOR SOMETHING
BIGGER. MAYBE IT'S TIME FOR SOME-
THING SMALLER. OR IT COULD BE
TIME TO WALK AWAY.

CHANGE IS FUCKING SCARY, BUT SO IS
STAYING IN A SPACE THAT NO LONGER
SERVES YOU. SO FIND THE FACES AND
PLACES THAT FIT YOU BEST.

STOP TRYING TO CHANGE YOU TO FIT INTO A SPACE THAT DOESN'T FIT YOU.

(SAME RULE GOES FOR PANTS.)

I'm the most content I've ever been, and do you know why? I threw away society's made-up expectations. I threw away the belief that getting more would make me more. I threw away the idea that being smaller would make me better. I stopped looking for happiness because I found out where it lives.

IT LIVES IN ME.

Contentment DOESN'T COME FROM ANYBODY OR ANYTHING ELSE.

Self-acceptance has to come from inside the skin suit. I can and will tell you I'm proud of you every day because you're still here, and that's an achievement. But bestie, you've gotta find the happiness inside your skin suit too.

WHEN I WAS 6 YEARS OLD, I asked if I could have a cupcake. I was told I could have it if I went outside for a walk or jog first because a cupcake was a treat that had to be earned. This was the first year I can remember thinking I was fat.

WHEN I WAS 12 YEARS OLD, I finally got the courage to wear a two-piece swimsuit. But before we left, I was singled out by my grandmother and told to change because I didn't have the body for that swimsuit. This was the first year I began actively restricting calories.

WHEN I WAS 19 YEARS OLD and a collegiate athlete, I met with my coach to go over my goals for the next season. My number one goal was to lose weight. I was silently begging for anybody to tell me my body was okay the way it was. But I was met with encouragement and agreement that this was a good idea. This was the year I began bingeing and purging and I dropped out of school twice.

WHEN I WAS 20 YEARS OLD, I recognized that nobody was coming to save me and I checked myself into inpatient treatment. My family vehemently tried to talk me out of this, saying that if I just exercised more I'd be able to eat again.

I saved myself but you should not have to be alone on your journey. If you think that it is not important to be celebrating bodies of all shapes and sizes, you're wrong.

YOUR BODY IS NOT A PROBLEM TO BE SOLVED. YOU NEED TO CHANGE THE CONVERSATION.

YOU DIDN'T TAKE THE WRONG PATH IN LIFE—THERE'S NO SET PATH. NOBODY IS KEEPING THE DIRECTIONS FROM YOU—THERE AREN'T ANY. NONE OF US HAVE THEM. YOUR GUIDEBOOK'S NOT MISSING PAGES—THERE JUST ISN'T A BOOK. STOP LOOKING FOR IT. YOU'RE HERE, AND IT'S NOW, SO GO WHERE YOU WANT TO GO. AND BE SURE TO TAKE THE SCENIC ROUTE ALONG THE WAY.

Hey, my body, while adorable, is the least interesting thing about me. Your body, also adorable, is the least interesting thing about you. The best parts of you and me are always here—good days, bad days, big pants, small pants—still me.

Stop waiting on your body to start living your life.

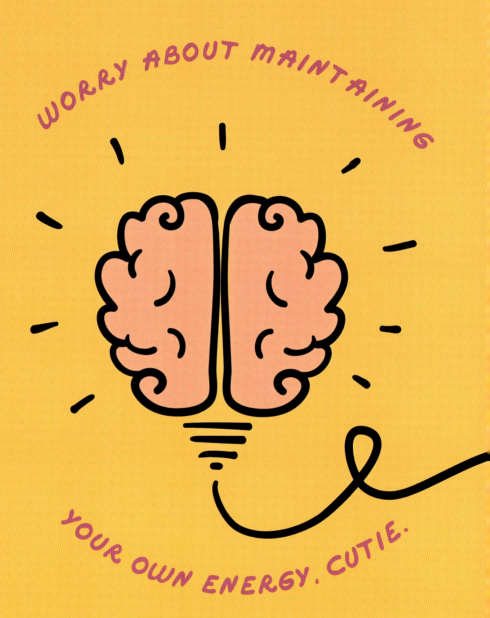

WORRY ABOUT MAINTAINING YOUR OWN ENERGY. CUTIE.

You cannot make everybody like you—it is just not possible. What somebody else thinks of you has nothing to do with you and every-thing to do with them.

Stop wasting all your energy on making everybody else happy but you. You're the only person you have any control over. STOP CARRYING AROUND ALL THAT NEGATIVE ENERGY FROM PEOPLE WHO AREN'T YOU.

Protect that tiny shred of peace that makes you whole, and let go of the expectations you think other people have for you. They don't have to live inside your brain and you do, so make it a nice place to live.

HEALING ISN'T LINEAR, AND SOMETIMES IT IS DOWNRIGHT SCARY. SOMETIMES YOUR BRAIN JUST WANTS TO GO BACK TO THE SPOOKY PLACES YOU'VE WORKED SO HARD TO CRAWL OUT OF.

But all the progress you've made before still exists. Taking a step back doesn't mean you didn't make all those kickass steps to heal.

You will get back there again, and you will move forward. Don't let one shitty setback wipe out all the love you've shown your head and your heart.

YOU KNOW WHAT ELSE

Little Hotties DO?

THEY GET OUT
THERE AND THEY

KICK
SOME
ASS.

CHAPTER 5

PROTECT YOUR PEACE

REMEMBER THAT YOU'RE THE ONLY PERSON THAT YOU HAVE CONTROL OVER, SO DON'T USE YOUR BRAIN, ENERGY, AND SPACE ON DING-DONGS.

You better find yourself a mirror,
look yourself dead in the eye,
and tell yourself you're a

MAGICAL CREATURE.

Have a jazzy day, my little jelly bean.

IF YOU NEED SOME ENCOURAGEMENT TODAY AND DON'T HAVE THE FAMILY YOU NEED, I'M HAPPY TO STEP IN. I LOVE YOUR IDENTITY AND I PROMISE TO RESPECT IT. I HAVE NO EXPECTATIONS OF YOU. I THINK YOU'RE EXACTLY WHERE YOU'RE SUPPOSED TO BE IN LIFE. I DON'T THINK YOU'RE BEHIND ON ANYTHING. I LOVE YOUR STYLE AND I THINK YOU'RE CUTE AS HECK. I LOVE WHATEVER WAY YOU'VE CHOSEN TO GO THROUGH LIFE. YOUR RELATIONSHIP STATUS IS ONLY MY BUSINESS IF YOU WANT IT TO BE. IF YOU'RE WALKING AWAY FROM A TOXIC RELATIONSHIP OR WORK SITUATION, I'M PROUD OF YOU.

JUST REMEMBER
THAT EVERY PART
OF YOU IS ENOUGH
RIGHT WHERE YOU
ARE, WHATEVER
YOU'RE DOING.

I DON'T SEE WHY THIS COULDN'T BE THE BEST DAY OF MY LIFE—THERE ARE NO RULES AGAINST IT. BUT I WOULD SETTLE FOR A DAY THAT DOESN'T MAKE ME WANNA CRY TOO. ANYTHING IN THAT RANGE IS FINE, REALLY. THANK YOU.

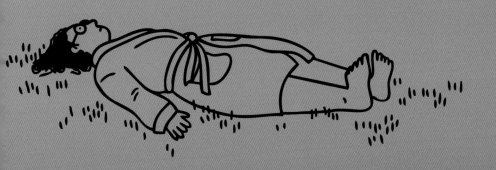

YOU'RE THE BEST!

IF YOU DON'T FEEL
SEEN AND HEARD, OR IF
YOU FEEL LIKE YOU'RE
LATE TO THE PARTY OR YOU
WERE NEVER INVITED TO
THE PARTY—GOOD! THROW
YOUR OWN PARTY.

BUILD A LIFE AND COMMUNITY AROUND YOURSELF THAT FITS. DON'T TRY TO JAM YOURSELF INTO A PARTY THAT ISN'T MEANT FOR YOU. WHY WOULD YOU WANT TO GO WHERE YOU DON'T FEEL WELCOME? STOP TRYING TO DO MORE TO FEEL WORTHY OF BEING INVITED. YOU'RE ALREADY WORTH IT. THERE IS A PARTY FOR YOU. THERE ARE PEOPLE OUT THERE WHO CAN SEE YOU AND HEAR YOU. YOU JUST MIGHT BE IN THE WRONG ROOM RIGHT NOW.

Are you filled with stress and anxiety and worry and fear about possibly making a change in your life? Open the door. Open the door to the big change. You don't have to cross the threshold.

Being able to see the big change takes away some of that fear. Opening the door lets some of that anxiety rush out. Don't let fear keep the door to change locked up tight.

NUDGE IT OPEN, BESTIE, AND LET *opportunity* COME KNOCKING.

EVERYBODY HAS

SO if you had your

AND GETTING OUT OF

TO LIFT A TON OF

and you're

a moldy hunk

YOU'RE NOT

AND IT'S JUST SOMETIMES

and it'll end

AND THERE'LL

VERY BAD DAYS

self a very bad day

BED WAS LIKE TRYING

BRICKS

thinking that you're

of bread...

IT'S NOT A GOOD DAY

BE OTHER DAYS

THERE IS A PERSON WHO NEEDS YOUR *love and affection* MORE THAN ANYBODY ELSE, AND THAT'S YOU.

Putting yourself first isn't selfish. Resting, self-care, and making yourself a priority isn't selfish—it's a necessity.

Of course it's nice to do cool stuff for other people. But if you've taken care of number one, you're gonna be so much better at it.

Stop denying yourself cool, awesome shit because you feel selfish for wanting it. Not only do you deserve it but you need it. *Now get out there and take care of you, cutie.*

CHAPTER 6

YOU ONLY HAVE 100%

YOU DON'T HAVE TO EARN REST. DID YOU KNOW THAT? YOU CAN SIMPLY NOT BE PRODUCTIVE IN YOUR FREE TIME. YOU DON'T EVEN HAVE TO FEEL GUILTY FOR RELAXING. YOU CAN JUST RELAX AND TRY TO ENJOY IT. RELAXING ISN'T A PRIZE FOR NOT RELAXING— IT'S JUST AN ACTIVITY THAT YOU CAN CHOOSE TO DO LIKE ANY OTHER ACTIVITY. YOU CAN JUST REST BECAUSE YOU WANT TO. DID I DO ANYTHING MORE TAXING THAN THE BARE MINIMUM TODAY? NO. DO I STILL DESERVE TO RELAX? YES, I DO. AND SO DO YOU.

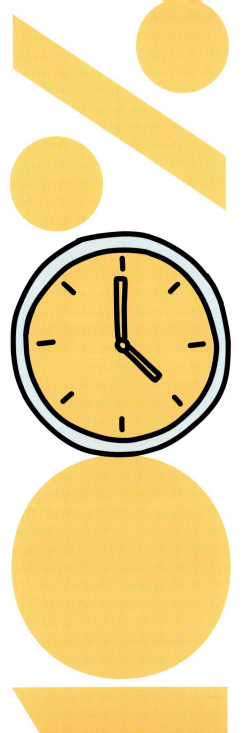

Stop trying to give multiple things in your life 100%. You only have 100%—that's a whole you. If you're giving multiple things in your life 100% of your effort, you're creating a deficit—burnout's coming, baby. Not everything deserves that much of you, I promise.

You cannot keep giving more than you have. Time to put a percentage on our obligations and priorities. And you best believe a big slice of that 100% pie had better be for rest.

If you think that life is an insufferable night-mare, run into the woods. Don't look back.

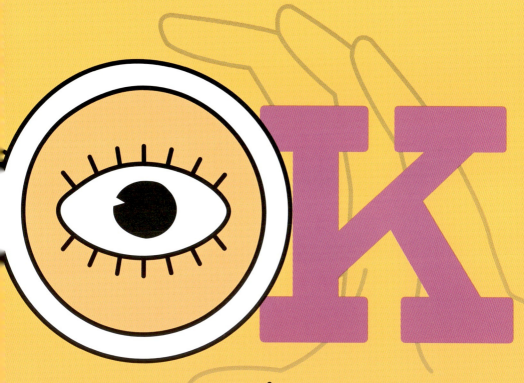

OK

for a bear with kind eyes.

Build a home together. The bear will teach you the ways of the woods. You'll teach him anxiety. Stay there forever.

EVERYTHING FEELS LIKE TOO MUCH RIGHT NOW. YOU'VE HIT YOUR LIMIT— YOUR WORKLOAD LIMIT, YOUR MENTAL LIMIT, YOUR EMOTIONAL LIMIT, YOUR SOCIAL LIMIT. ME TOO.

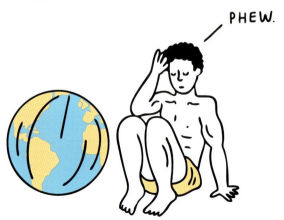

PHEW.

If you can't quite pinpoint what is wrong but everything feels a thousand times heavier than usual, it's a sign from your body and brain that it's time to recharge.

We require rest—not just physical rest, but *mental* and *emotional* rest.

We cannot power through our entire lives and expect our bodies to just take it. We run out of gas too. Take time and space—you need it.

I DON'T HAVE IT IN ME TODAY TO DO TODAY. I DON'T HAVE THE PATIENCE OR THE ENERGY OR THE MOTIVATION. SO I WANT TO DO NO THINGS. MAYBE I'LL JUST SIT IN THE SUN AND HAVE A LITTLE MAC AND CHEESE, OKAY? THANK YOU.

Are you feeling lost? Like you don't really know how you feel, but it's definitely not good in there? Like there are so many things that need you to do them that you're frozen in place? Or maybe you are kind of on autopilot because that's all you can handle right now? That's okay.

You cannot expect your brain to run in overdrive constantly and not burn the fuck out. Take a minute. Even a machine, a robot, a computer gets to power down every once in a while. Do you think your smooshy brain is tougher than a metal machine? No, bestie, it's not.

Give it a rest.

TAKE A BREATHER.
FOCUS ON JUST
STAYING ALIVE RIGHT
NOW—AND IF THAT'S
ALL YOU'VE GOT,
THAT'S PLENTY.

THERE'S SO MUCH PRESSURE to be a go-getter who can do it all. You don't have to do more to be more. You know what I want to be more of? More happy. More fulfilled. More rested.

STOP WASTING ALL YOUR PRECIOUS TIME and energy doing more to feel like you're more, and start doing less. Do less of what makes you miserable. Less of what doesn't bring value to your life. Do less of the shit that drains you.

There are only so many things that are worthy of your time. Do less to be more of the stuff that matters.

BAD DAY REMINDER

YOUR PRODUCTIVITY IS NOT A MEASURE OF YOUR VALUE. YOUR SIZE IS NOT A MEASURE OF YOUR VALUE. YOUR FINANCES ARE NOT A MEASURE OF YOUR VALUE. YOU'RE ALREADY VALUABLE, BESTIE.

All these feelings
but I wish
So I could just feel
like an

that doesn't have
it's protected by

So it's just a

122

are coming in waves

they didn't

regular all the time

inland lake

waves because mountains

little calmer

I KNOW YOU HAVE A TO-DO LIST A MILE LONG AND YOUR GUILT IS GROWING FASTER THAN A WEED, BUT IF YOU ARE RUN-DOWN AND YOUR BODY IS SCREAMING FOR REST—GO REST. WHEN YOUR PHONE RUNS OUT OF BATTERY, IT DOESN'T FEEL GUILTY OR ASK FOR PERMISSION; IT JUST SAYS, "BYE, BESTIE," AND GOES TO SLEEP. REST IS REQUIRED. THE LAUNDRY WILL ALWAYS BE THERE, AND THE DISHES ARE NOT RUNNING AWAY WITH THE SPOON. SO TELL YOUR GUILT TO BUZZ OFF AND PUT IT ON THE BACK BURNER. REST, MY SWEET ANGEL MUFFIN. YOU DESERVE TO RECHARGE.

CHAPTER 7

GIVE 'EM THE RAZZLE FUCKING DAZZLE

I NEED MY BRAIN TO STOP BULLYING ME INTO BELIEVING THAT I'M A USELESS SACK OF MOLDY OLD BEANS. I'D LIKE TO REMEMBER THAT I AM AS MAGICAL AS A BALL OF MOZZARELLA, AND I AM IN FACT A KICKASS LITTLE HOTTIE WHO IS VERY CAPABLE OF GETTING OUT THERE AND GIVING THEM THE RAZZLE FUCKING DAZZLE, OKAY? THANK YOU.

Wins are wins, bestie.

Stop getting down on yourself because you think you haven't achieved great things. Listen, the losses will come. Celebrate all the wins.

DID YOU GET OUT
OF BED TODAY?

WELL
DONE!

DID YOU BRUSH
YOUR TEETH TODAY?

CHANGE YOUR
PANTS TODAY?

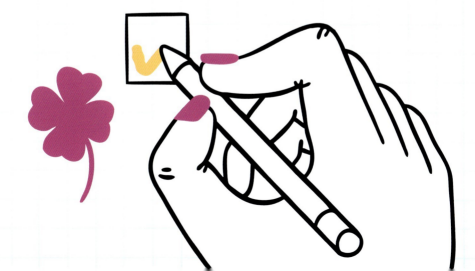

Are you a people pleaser?

Last I checked you're a people,
but I suspect that you're not the
person you're trying to please.

Please your own damn self,
people. You come first. The
only person whose opinion
about you matters is yours.

I BETTER CATCH
YOU BEING
NICE AS HECK
TO YOURSELF
TODAY.

HEY, COULD I STOP WAITING FOR THE OTHER SHOE TO DROP EVERY TIME SOMETHING GOOD OR COOL HAPPENS? INSTEAD, COULD I JUST BE LIKE "WOW, THIS IS SO GOOD AND COOL"? OKAY? THANK YOU.

IT'S CALLED MANIFESTING— LOOK IT UP.

There's no deadline for figuring out your identity. It's totally fine to change your mind on what's next for you. It's okay to never know what you want to be when you grow up. Sometimes *finding* *yourself* is just remembering who you were before the entire world told you who you should be.

I BETTER NOT CATCH YOU BEATING YOURSELF UP TODAY BECAUSE YOU'RE STRUGGLING MENTALLY. EVERY DAY YOUR BRAIN COMES AT YOU, FISTS UP, AND YET YOU'RE STILL OUT HERE, EXISTING UP A STORM. AND YOU'RE NOT GONNA BE FRUSTRATED WITH YOURSELF, MY KICKASS FRIEND, BECAUSE YOUR BRAIN IS MIS-WIRED. RIGHT NOW YOU BETTER TELL YOURSELF YOU'RE A KICKASS LITTLE HOTTIE. TELL YOUR BRAIN TO BUZZ OFF. QUIT BEATING YOURSELF UP. LIFE IS HARD ENOUGH WITHOUT YOUR OWN SELF ATTACKING YOU. YOU'RE ENOUGH JUST THE WAY YOU ARE.

YOU'RE MORE *kickass* THAN YOU EVEN KNOW.

It's time for our "me" season: a season
for not getting stuck in one lane.
Time to wear what we want.

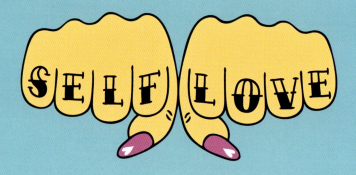

Time to eat things that make our
belly and our brain smile. Time to
break out of our fear bubble.
It's our time for bravery.

I'M SICK OF LIVING
SCARED, AND I'M SICK
OF LIVING STUCK. TIME
TO RISE FROM THE
FRICKIN' ASHES OF BEING
BURNED OUT, BESTIE.
IT'S MOTHERFUCKIN'
ME TIME.

Give yourself permission to breathe. If you won't do it, I'm telling you: Take a breath. Why are you striving so hard for perfection over there? Has anything been perfect before? No. 'Cause nothing is ever perfect, and something always happens. That's a fact of life. Don't wait to enjoy things because they're not perfect.

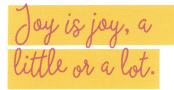

Joy is joy, a little or a lot.

ENJOY WHAT YOU CAN, WHEN YOU CAN.

Did you hear that, cutie? It's motherfucking ME time and motherfucking YOU time. I hope the words on these pages bring you a little respite on the hard days, a laugh on the long days, and a pep talk on the days you are down.

GET OUT THERE AND GIVE 'EM THE OLD RAZZLE FUCKING DAZZLE.

AND YOU KNOW
YOU BETTER
KEEP IT UP, CUTIE.
I'M SO PROUD
OF YOU.

First published in the United States of America in 2024 by
Rizzoli Universe
A Division of Rizzoli International Publications, Inc.
300 Park Avenue South
New York, NY 10010
www.rizzoliusa.com

Publisher: Charles Miers
Associate Publisher: James Muschett
Editor: Dinah Dunn, Indelible Editions
Design: Andrea Duarte, Indelible Editions
Production Manager: Colin Hough Trapp
Managing Editor: Lynn Scrabis
Editorial Review: Elizabeth Smith

Produced by Indelible Editions

Printed in China

2024 2025 2026 2027 / 10 9 8 7 6 5 4 3 2 1

ISBN: 978-0-7893-4418-2
Library of Congress Control Number: 2023940902

SHUTTERSTOCK.COM:
1001holiday, 85; ArtMari, 74;
Alina Beketova, 22; Bibadash,
96; cosmaa, 83; Devita ayu
silvianingtyas, 86; DreamLoud,
102; Seth Gallmeyer, 6, 32;
Gwens Graphic Studio, 37, 80;
Irmun, 25; lil_smasher23, 88;
mhatzapa, 38, 64-65; nickfz,
6; nikiteev_konstantin, 106;
Paket, 142; Ramcreative, 112-113;
Tatgynsy, 136; Polina Tomtosova,
84; VectorPlotnikoff, 55; Irina
Voziyan, 106

IT'S CALLED MANIFESTING—LOOK IT UP

WINS ARE WINS

Bestie

TRY TO HAVE SOME FUN

KEEP IT UP, CUTIE

BE A KICKASS *little* HOTTIE

Don't Be A SHITTY *Person*

Have a jazzy day, my little jelly bean

GET OUT THERE AND GIVE 'EM THE OLD RAZZLE FUCKING DAZZLE